My Life in
Poetry

Donald Suckstorff

My Life in Poetry

LitPrime Solutions
21250 Hawthorne Blvd
Suite 500, Torrance, CA 90503
www.litprime.com
Phone: 1-800-981-9893

Published by LitPrime Solutions   05/24/2023

ISBN: 979-8-88703-181-1(sc)
ISBN: 979-8-88703-182-8(hc)
ISBN: 979-8-88703-183-5(e)

Library of Congress Control Number: 2023903806

Foreword

I started to write in 1974, this book is a compilation of poems that I have written over the years. Each and every poem in this book comes from my heart in some way. They have all been a part of my life at one time or another. Therefore, they are true to me, and thus the title *My Life in Poetry*. There are many people and incidents from my life that have inspired me to write these poems. I wish to thank all those that have inspired me and especially God for allowing me the ability to write in this manner.

I thought very hard about whether or not to write an expletive for each poem to let the reader know what I felt and thought during these times. However, I decided that each person that reads this book should find their own meaning and questions that arise. Therefore, I give you my heart and mind. I ask that you consider each and every poem carefully and find the value in it yourself. I truly hope that you enjoy reading this book as much as I have put it together. There were many tears shed in writing this book and smiles as well. Life is different for all of us. My only hope is that I have given something in this book that you will find valuable to you. Thank you for the opportunity to share my thoughts and feelings with you.

Contents

A Friend I Adore

I have a friend that I adore
We have never met
But she's a friend for sure

Our friendship grew on the internet
We can talk for hours
Without a worry or a fret

We talk to each other everyday
We share our joy and pain
Then we wonder out loud what will come our way

Even if we never meet face to face
Our relationship will flourish
With dignity and grace

A Vision of Beauty

The majestic mountains stood so high
With their snow-capped peaks reaching for the sky
The pine trees stood so tall
It was a miracle that they did not fall

The Falcons and Eagles soared high above
This is when I knew nature was a real love
The water running down so pure and cold
From melting snow and springs, a lot of natural beauty to behold

The bushes, the creatures, all of nature to see
If I open my eyes and really look it is not hidden from me
There is a smell of freshness all around me
It is something I have never taken the time to see

For on this day I took a walk
Through the wilderness that was put here for me
It is a world I have never taken the time to see
Because I was always so busy just thinking of me

All Alone

I feel shrouded in darkness when I am alone
This is my life, even at home
My heart is as empty as the cupboards are bare
The rooms are all vacant I just sit here and stare
Do I have any friends, if so do they care?
My phone does not ring; no one knocks at my door
Is this what life is, shouldn't there be more?
My eyes start to water, there is a lump in my throat
I choke back the tears, and then my eyes start to float
I realize I'm lonely, boy does it hurt
My heart races wildly, and my head spins
Why must I feel so much pain and hurt?

Alone

The night has come and the day has ended

The darkness preempts the light from above

The stars shine brightly as ever before

The light from the distant ships flickers and dances ever so smoothly

Glistening on the oceans water

The faint salty smell lingers in the cool summer air

I look over the shore and all that I see

Are the lights from the buildings not too distant from me

Looking out from the beach as far as I can see

The sky is like the ocean, deep, dark, and whispering to me

The sky and the ocean are endless, or so it seems

Beauty

The beauty of a rose
Is indeed a pleasure
However
Your beauty
By far
Out measures

Breathless

When I saw you lying on the grass
I had images of an Angel from my past
Your smile was soft and you were not crass
Your demure and beauty far surpassed

When you raised your head and looked at me
It was remarkable what I could see
Your brown eyes sparkled like a million stars
Making me feel as though I was on a trip to mars

I could not remove my eyes from yours
They beckoned me in as if taking a tour
I saw your heart as it opened for me
I felt how warm your love would be

The rose in your cheeks and your wonderful smile
Lent me strength to walk the longest mile
I could not see any imperfection in you
Because God had made the perfect you

Courage

There is courage, it takes to stand alone
We very seldom ever acknowledge it
Simply put, that person is out of the norm
Yet they stand for their belief
And in their own way ready to fight

Most never really understand
They stand for their belief and right
The majority are ready to condemn
Instead of taking a moment and trying to understand

Do you know what it is to stand alone?
You call them nuts never giving them a rest
And all they are doing is trying to be their best

America was founded as the land of the free
But for some reason the majority
Will just not let it be

Daddy, Please Come Home

The news is on every night at home
The family watches with a serious tone
I am still not sure what it all means
And my daddy's not here to explain it to me

My daddy's in the Army
And that's what is on TV
They are talking about dying
And how brave these men must be

I see people lying all around on the ground
My mommy has tears running from her eyes
I give her a hug and a kiss
Then I say mommy don't cry

She hugs me squeezing me tight
She says don't worry honey it will be alright
Daddy will be home soon
Everything will be alright

Feeling

The colors in a rainbow are very bright
Like the sparkle in your eyes light up my night
The sound of your voice is sweet to hear
It is just like music to my ear
The warmth I feel when you are near
Let's me know I have nothing to fear

Feeling Empty

I have this emptiness inside of me
My heart does not feel whole
My mind will not let it be
I always wonder what it will take to make it whole

I thought I knew what it would take
But then I can never be sure
I have always been looking for my heart's sake
But all I have ever found was a temporary cure

I wish to lift my spirit high
To feel the love, I know is there
My tears to stop and no longer cry
There is one that I can make it so, but where

Is my patience wearing thin?
Am I looking too hard trying to find?
Hoping that my heart will win
Or is it all just a figment of my mind

Forever Love

I have never loved
The way that I love you
My heart is broken
In more pieces than two
My heart will be yours
Forever and a day
This I cannot change
Nor would I ever want to

Friends

Friends may come

Friends may go

You my friend

Should always know

For you my heart

Has a special glow

Guardians of The Night

We are the few, the proud, and the patriotic
We spend many nights in the dark alone
The world has always been very chaotic
We do not know what to expect
So we will walk the night to protect
Our God, our country, and our home

The ones we love and our fellow countrymen
Are tucked away in their beds
And nestled in their warm homes
We will walk our post no matter the weather
And try to fight our feelings of being all alone

At times our feet will freeze
Our bodies will shiver
And our hands will feel numb
We continue to walk the beaten path
And pray that nothing goes wrong

We are one of the lowest-paid workers
And our duty is twenty-four hours long
We will walk our post in silence
Until our relief comes to carry on
We do not ask much and we very seldom feel loved

For most, it is a calling
And a job we know must be done
So we put ourselves on the first line
With the thought of keeping you safe at home
Because we are the Guardians of the night

Gift from My Heart

When I give a gift from my heart
Especially to someone that I never knew
I do it selfishly
From my own point of view

The feeling I get I cannot describe
Just to know that it touched them so much inside
It makes me so happy and warm inside

When I see the look on their face
And the tears in their eyes.
Sometimes, all I can do is cry

So when I say that I do it selfishly
It is because of the warmth
And happiness that washes over me
It is my memory to last an eternity

I cannot believe how easy it is
To restore a smile and touch a heart
By some small thing
I do from my heart

Goodbye My Brother

A Soldiers Fear

I'm tired of today and afraid of tomorrow
I'm not happy with the past and fear the future
I found that I have never really known love it is not my friend
I'm eighteen and too young to die

The world is not what I had hoped it to be
There is too much pain and anger for me
As I reflect on these thoughts,
The dark sky suddenly burst into flames
Bullets fly all around me I am hiding in vain

My fear level is very high
The noises and screams of anguish are too much to hear
They fall deaf upon my ear
The stench of death is very near
It is coming for me is my greatest fear

Soon it's quiet and the darkness is here
The screams are all that I can hear
I am still alive and smothered in fear

If you were to ask me where I have been
I could only tell you I have lost my friends
I cannot speak of that world tonight
Because for me it is full of fright

My friends had left me one fateful night
Leaving me with this tiring fight
I shall always know they are not far away
For in my heart is where they always stay

Happy Valentines

To the love of my life
On this special day
My love for you
Shall never fade away
It grows stronger
Each and every day

I could not imagine life
If you ever went away
My heart I pledge to you
And give myself in every way

Although this is Valentine's Day
I want you to know
To me, you are special
Each and every day

Her Smile

She has the most beautiful smile I have ever seen
When her lips curl up, her eyes have a special gleam
Surrounded by mystery and very shy
She has a look that is mystic, and very wry
Her voice is so quiet and very hard to hear
Yet you feel something special, whenever she's near
Her smile catches you unaware
For some reason, you stop and stare
When your eyes meet, you feel as though she sees in your soul
Taken by such surprise, all you can do is smile, and say hello

Heroes of the World

What drives a person to be so bold
To give their life to save another
That they will never know

One can only reflect
On what it must be
Because most of us
We shall never see

And those that do
Shall never tell
The secret went with them
When they fell

Life is precious
There is no guarantee
Live it to the fullest
You never know what will be

I Am Not So Different

Why do you ridicule and laugh at me?
It is only the outside that you see
But I have a heart and I feel inside
The things on the outside I cannot hide
I am different then you, this is true
But my malady is nothing new
When will people have a different view?
Will they ever see me for who I am?
That on the inside I am the same as them
My body is crippled or my mind is maimed
I shall never have a fortune or reach any fame
But God will love me, just the same
Why can't you just reach out and remember my name?
Hug me and help me, shed some pain
Our souls were all made, to be the same

I Knew

From the moment we first talked I knew
When I first laid eyes upon you
It was then again that I knew

When our lips first touched I knew
When I felt your heart beating against mine
It was then again that I knew

When we made love for the first time I knew
When you walked out my door
It was then again that I knew

That I want to spend the rest of my life with you

I Never Knew

I treated you the best I could
Better than most ever would
But still, I ask what went wrong
It is never as easy as it sounds in a song

I love you more than I ever knew I could
Is there something I have not done that I should?
I would like to know if it is just me
Or is it just what was meant to be

I have spent my life looking for love
I found it once, but she was taken by God above
Then I found you and I thought it was true
Now my heart is broken and again I am blue

Love cannot be a one-sided affair
So I ask myself why I still care
There is one thing I need to know
Then maybe I can heal and start letting go

Inner Strength

You are the strongest woman I have ever met
You face everyday life and have cheated death
Your voice wavers but you keep a very strong hold
You are a little sassy but you are very bold

I do not think you know your inner strength
Or the ability you have to go the length
You say your life is a mess and you have fear
Yet you cope with it all and life is so dear

If you could only see yourself as I do
The smile on your face each day anew
The sparkle in your eyes that lights up the room
The bounce in your step, never succumbing to gloom

From you we can all learn something I'm sure
Your heart and thoughts are so very pure
How lucky I am that God has shared you with me
If you were not so hard on yourself then maybe this, you could see

Insecure

Why is it I cannot see?
When everyone is looking at me
What is it deep inside?
That I obviously cannot hide
Is there something that shows through me?
That tells them all that I am not worthy
Or is it just me, feeling my insecurity

Inside Out

Wouldn't it be great if people saw the inside first?
Have you ever wondered why we see the outside in?
Maybe we would realize we all have the same thirst
When we smile inevitably it is all called a grin

Does the shell make the person?
Or does it all come from within
We were all made differently for a reason
When we only see the outside isn't it really a sin

Maybe the children should be teaching us
Instead of us teaching them
If only you watch them, you will see what is just
The only hatred they have is what we have given them

The next time you look try to look within
Because if all you see is fat, thin, ugly, or the color of the skin
If all you see is crippled or a malformed grin
Then you my friend are the one that is full of sin

Life

Life has never been the way I thought it should be
It is full of disappointment and heartache for me
I walk through the day and force a smile for those I see
While deep inside I fear my life will never be pain-free

I often wonder if I am the only one that must force a smile
It seems I can even fool those that have known me for a while
The outward appearance is all you see, what I feel inside I save for me
The wall I built is mine you see; only I can decide how strong it will be

So you think I am happy because you see me smile
But inside I walk many treacherous miles
Sometimes the hills seem so long and steep
By the time I reach the top, there are blisters all over my feet

Why do I fight so hard to get by?
When I know that in the end
I will surely die

Life for Me

Everyday life seems so hard to me
Sometimes I wish I were a tree
I would not have to worry about the clothes I wear
I would not even have to comb my hair

Do I worry too much about how I look?
Will I meet the standards of society's book?
I try so hard to fit the mold
Here I am just growing old

Why do we focus on the outside so much?
When the real beauty is in the touch
Will I ever grow up and understand?
More importantly, it's the way you hold my hand

There is no beauty on the outside of me
Within my soul and my heart, is the tree
I am filled with love and nourishment
But in my mind, I am not content

The wisdom and strength you will not see
Unless you take the time to look at me

Love

Unconditional love
It never ends
It's so hard to find
Even in friends

If you find it
And it is true
You shall always have it
No matter what you do

They may not always
Approve of what you do
But the reality is
They will always love you

It is a love
That never seeks change
But supports
And accepts you

Where is it hidden
Where can it be found
This truly is a mystery
But we all love the sound

So if you are lucky

And this you have found

You must always remember

To turn the love around

Loving You

You are my life, my daily bread
From you I receive nourishment
For the road ahead
Since I have fallen in love with you
My entire life has been renewed
Sometimes it is hard for me to say
How much I really love you, each and every day
I want you to know what you mean to me
If you could look into my mind
Then you would see
I think of you constantly
Each day the little things I see in you
Renews my love and keeps it true
Your eyes make me melt when you look into mine
When I gaze at you I lose track of time
We were brought together by God above
For you are the one that I cherish and love

Make a Difference

It has been said that one person cannot make a difference
I challenge these critics and I say nay
You can make a difference for one person
Each and every day

No one else can do what it is you do
Because we are all unique
And this I know to be true

If you make a change in one person's life
They will go out and touch the next
So make a small difference in someone's life

Their smile will surely warm your heart
This I know from doing my part
And it surely will be a very nice start

Man's Frailty

My heart throbbed when our lips met
Your kiss took me away without any regrets
My anticipation grew as the day lingered on
Soon it would be night and the thoughts of this place would be gone

When you came to me
It was my heart you would break
To you, it was a game
To pass time until you wake

Why did you come to me?
In this dreadful place
If your intentions were not to keep a smile on my face

Promises you made with no intention to keep
I will lay down on my head unable to sleep
I will have visions and dreams only of you
My heart will feel sad but in life it is true

Again I fell for the oldest line
But a new you

Morning Glory

I walked through the woods with the morning dew
The trees were thick but in spots the sun shone through
I climbed the hill to the highest peak
It was the morning glory that I did seek

I looked to the east over the next hill
The vision I saw was a wondrous thrill
The purple, the orange, and the shades of blue
The sun was rising unsettling the morning dew

The silence started to break as the Forest came alive
Birds started chirping the morning had arrived
With the sun came warmth I felt on my face
Unlike the crowded city here there was no race

The wilderness awoke and started to move
It appeared to move slowly with a constant groove
The odors, the colors, all the natural beauty
Gave light to the mountain's natural serenity

My All

To me you are everything
Winter, summer, fall, and especially spring
My life would mean nothing if it were not for you
My love for you is very true
I want to hold you on this lonely night
But I know your world is full of fright
My love for you is very true
I know to believe that is hard for you
Please don't leave me all alone
For I know together we can make a beautiful home

My Angel

Your momma left when you were three
I knew that you and your little sister would be depending on me
My world had shattered and I was not sure what to do
I was sitting in my bedroom crying my eyes out
Feeling like my heart had been torn from me
You walked into my room and pushed your way between my knees
You looked up at me so proud and smart
You said "daddy, don't cry I will always be here to take care of you"
I took you into my arms and squeezed you so tight
I knew my little three-year-old baby was my guardian angel tonight
For the next three years, things were rough
Whenever I felt I could not deal with it I just thought of you
Over the past twenty-six years, life has thrown a lot at me
Whenever it seems unbearable I just think of you
Thinking of you makes all my troubles seem so small
Because there you are standing so tall at just three years old
Time has a way of making things change
There is one thing that will always stay the same
That is you being my little girl

My Christmas Day

Here I sit on Christmas day
I cry for Jesus to come my way
I am all alone and my house is empty
I have no one that has asked me to share their day

Then I feel Jesus is in my heart
I know from me, He will never part
Somehow the sadness starts to lift
I find in my heart a special gift

I look out the window and there I see
Another lonely soul waiting for me
I asked them to come in and share my day
I take them by the hand and show them the way

Through the dirt on their faces and the smell of their clothes
I saw the most wonderful smile, and it was not a pose
I offered a shower and some clean clothes
I made myself busy setting the table and I placed a rose

I got out the bread, some chips, and an old can of spam
I smiled nervously and said, "we can pretend this is ham."
The stranger smiled and said, "this is a feast for a king.
Angels will look over you and you will hear them sing."

For the gift, you have given me on this Christmas day
You shall be rewarded forever and a day
You have opened your heart and your home
From this day forward you shall never be alone

With a hug and smile the stranger had gone
I felt as though I had riches though there were none
I no longer felt so lonely and poor
For God's gift to me was an open heart and door

My Christmas Wish

Do you remember when?
The star shone brightly over Bethlehem
The three Kings rode night and day
To pay homage to a newborn babe lying in the hay
Do you still remember that this was God's gift?
To wash our sins away and give our souls a lift
This is the time for us to rejoice
Because Jesus was born to give us a choice
Do you really understand the meaning of the day?
Or is it just about the gifts and how much we will pay
I ask you to consider those in need
For Jesus was not given selfishly
Pray to God on this very day
Thank the Lord for the gift we received
And ask your heart
What would he like from me?

My Heart

Your beauty cannot be measured
By the outside alone
When I gaze into your eyes
I see the beauty within
It is not for all men to see
You are the most beautiful woman to me
I'm held captive by your essence
And the warmth I see
My heart is yours if you wish it to be
After being with you
My heart could never again wander free

My Little Brick Room

Here I sit in my little brick room

Safe, secure, and hidden from doom

You cannot come in or see my room

I do not like to share

I have no trust in you

My heart has been broken

I felt the pain

I cannot believe what you say to me

I have heard it before

It is all the same

You say you are different

You could not possibly be

So do not get

Close to me

My Loss

Her eyes were warm and full of fire
They captured my heart and brought forth my desire
Her beauty and aura kept me in awe
I knew this was the most beautiful woman
I ever saw
I tried to speak but I could only stammer
I felt she could never love me in any way or manner

My Love for Thee

The warmth and love you have shown me
Has become my living tree
As each branch grows strong and bold
I hope for you to ever hold
I did not foresee the weak branch break
As I placed the weight and put everything at stake
The branch can grow and be strong again
If it will be allowed to nurture and mend

I broke your heart this is true
But I never intended on hurting you
My love for you is big and bold
I hope for you to ever hold
If you will allow me to mend your heart
I promise from you I will never part

Our love can mend like the tree
But only if you allow it to be
It will be stronger and bolder forever for thee

My Mind

I often wonder what it is I see
Is life my own or is it destined to be
The tapes in my head are from my past
Do they guide me and shape my destiny?
Do I believe what they tell me no matter what I see?
Are my past relationships ruling me?
I have found the love for me
My tapes will not allow it to be
My mind tells me that it can't be good for me
Yet I know this is the best for me
Am I so blind that I cannot see?
This person's love is true for me
Yet I won't bend because my mind tells me
It's all the same and always will be

My Mom

I never really knew how much I would miss you
And then you were gone
You were my confidant, the one I talked to
Whenever things went wrong

I will never understand how we ever got so close
Because I had so many resentments all along
I never really felt that you were on my side
I had such a hard time trying to find where I belonged

I tried to do everything I could to make your life good
The one thing that I could never really do
Was to show my unconditional love to you
For some reason, I always thought that it should be different

Then when you died my world shattered
I felt so alone and felt like I no longer had a home
I was two thousand miles away
And did not find out until the end of the day

I cried all night and the pain would not go away
It was then I realized
You gave your love in a very unselfish way
I drove hard all the next day
Trying not to cry so I could find my way

You left a letter for all to read
It was then that I realized my real need
I never thought that I could be so wrong
It was my need to be forgiven all along

My Nightmare

The nightmares continue to follow me
When I look in the mirror this I see
I feel ashamed of what is staring at me
I wish I could make it different but it is not to be

War is my tormentor and on that, we can agree
But will you ever understand what has happened to me
I am not so sure that even I can clearly see
All I know is that I am ashamed of me

We were never there so it could not be true
Yet my heart is so cold and I feel so blue
I have the images in my mind
Of the ones that were left far behind

We did not do what we knew we should
I am not sure we tried everything we could
But war is hell and of this, you can be sure
I will search my mind forever to find my own cure

I will never forget and the images will never disappear
Sometimes in my dreams, I will relive the fear
I fight with myself in the darkness of night
Just trying to decide if what I did was right

My Thoughts

In my thinking, am I vain?
What is my purpose?
What is my name?
I am lost and all alone
I am looking for my home
I don't think I can make it alone
I need someone to hold me
And make me feel at home
Do not feel bad
That I am sad
For the pain in life is all
I have ever known

My Time

When my time is up and it surely will be
I will hope my love was there for all to see
I will be remembered for my heart and not gold
My greatest reward was growing old

It is unfortunate that I do not feel human love
The only love I feel in me is given by God above
I crave the love of a human touch
Then I wonder am I asking too much?

I have been blessed in many ways
But yet I crave what I cannot sway
I would give all that I own
For peace in my heart and to not feel alone

It seems to me this will never be
So I continue to give, this is free
It saddens me that the world is so cold
I will share all my warmth if I can remain so bold

My Valentine

The sight of you takes my breath away
My heart flutters and my mind begins to stray
Your sweet smell drives me crazy in every way
Won't you be mine this Valentine's Day?

My Word

If a man is a man, a contract he will not need
My word is my power and my riches indeed
If a promise is made, then it must be fulfilled
If it is money you want, then send me a bill

To have dignity in me this is real
The treasures I have are what I am able to feel
With a smile and warm touch, this is how I greet
To share my love with all that I meet

My heart is big and giving to all
If you are in need just give me a call
If I can help, then it shall be done
The world has been changed by the victors of one

To give myself is the greatest of all
Touching a heart can make a wall fall
I can find money all around
Without someone to love, I am truly bound

My World

Life seems hard enough without always feeling confused
I always think that I know what I am getting into
But then I usually end up feeling as though I have been used
Then I wonder why I have put myself into this position
When I know that this is not unique or new

I give my love fully without putting conditions on you
Then I must think that this is something
That I really should not do
How many times will it take before I do something new

Maybe it looks as though I am the idiot of the world
But I do not think I would ever change who or what I am
This is who I am in my world
And I know I shall put myself there again

National Cemetery

The stone cold marble at my feet

Make my eyes water and I begin to weep

My brothers surround me from wars before

They whisper from their graves

They shall march no more

My heart is heavy

My soul feels cold

I can see my brothers march to their death

So brave and so bold

It is if I was standing

That very day

On that very knoll

I feel the pain from that terrible day

My heart cries loudly

I cannot stay

I stand proudly and salute you

Before I turn to walk away

Nothing Left

It seems as though you want so much from me
I feel most of the time that I have nothing left to give
My heart is worn, battered and torn
Most days I do what I can just to live

I am a bankrupt emotional wreck
I have traveled this road before
But this time it's different
My heart does not seem to restore

My heart has lost its rhythmic beat
I am not sure what there is to do
It feels as though it lies at my feet
I feel as though there is no measure of repair

My heart cannot take this anymore
I cannot allow my heart to feel
I think it is time to close the door
This time the pain is forever real

Our Love

I want to hold your body close to mine
So that you may feel my heart beat all the time
As our hearts beat together they soon will rhyme
Our love will grow forever and be suspended in time

The way we feel will grow stronger each day
As we work together to make our way
We will work together and toil each day
To make our love stronger in every way

We will have an eternity for us to show
How great our love is and how much it can grow
For our love will be stronger than anyone could possibly know

Perspectives

I looked into your eyes
There I did see
The blue of the ocean
I could feel your serenity

I wish I could see the world as you do
You seem so happy
I am so blue

Is there a secret
Hidden in you
Can you tell me
I want it too

Is it something you have
Or something you do
The world would be so happy
If only we knew

You see the good
I see the bad
You see the happy
I see the sad

You see with your heart
I see with my head
You smile each day
Each day I dread

Rekindled Heart

For so long I thought my heart was imprisoned
That love for me would never be
You came along and captured my heart
Literally setting it free

You made my heart sing
Causing my mind to dance
Now my body moves in harmony

From this day forward I shall be yours
For you have lit the flame
Now my fire forever roars

The challenges ahead will be great I know
But I would swim the widest river
Climb the highest mountain
Just to reach my destiny

The years to come will surely show
Your love has captured all of me

Seeing You

When at first I saw you from afar
You were as bright as a shining star
Now that we are closer
I have gotten to know you
Your beauty and aura
Can by far
Outshine any star

Self

If I look deep into my soul
Will I find there is a hole?
If I died today
Would the hole go away?
Have I lived my life to the fullest it could be?
Have I been true to me?
Been the best I could possibly be
Did I help my fellow man?
In every way, I possibly can
These are questions I must ask
To know if I have fulfilled my task
When it comes that judgment day
Will I know what I must pay?

September 11th 2001

My heart is heavy
So many have died
September 11th 2001
The day without pride
We must pray
Then bury our dead
Life must go on
We must move ahead
We will never forget
Those that died
We must continue
To show our pride
Those that have fallen
Belong to our family
They are not forgotten
They will be remembered daily
This day September 11th 2001
Shall live in history

Silence

The sound of silence is my old friend
It has always been with me
And shall be until the end
The one thing that's certain
And I know for sure
I can only count on myself for more
I thought people were different
But they are all the same
As the fire flickers and this, I see
This might be the only warmth
That's destined for me

Since You

Since the very first day that I fell for you
It is the only thing that I have ever wanted to do
Just to keep you close to me
For the rest of my life

Now I can't seem to get you off my mind
Even though it has been a very long time
All I can think of is loving you

When I wake up in the morning and open my eyes
Everything is still the same there is no surprise
Then I wonder if I can go on this way
Just wish and hope for you
To call me and to hear you say
I love you and I want you to come back home

I can't seem to get you out of my mind
And it's been two damn years

I'll try getting over you
Because I know it's something that I've got to do
I never thought I could feel so blue
Especially not this way over you
But the hurt won't go away
It just keeps pounding me harder every day

So I get up and try to work you off my mind
I try to clean out all the memories
But it seems I just can't bring myself to throw your pictures away
Several ladies want to be by my side
And God knows that I've tried
But I can't seem to get you out of my mind
And it's been two damned years

Time has taken its toll on my heart
But I have to wonder if you ever loved me from the start
Here I am, just another broken heart
And I feel myself dying a little each day
It doesn't seem to matter how much I pray

I just can't seem to get you out of my mind
No! I can't seem to get you
Out of my mind...

Sorry Isn't Worth It Anymore

I don't believe I could love someone
The way I loved you
You treated my heart like a play toy
Doing things, you do
You broke my heart and said I'm sorry
That has always worked for you
For nine long years, I listened to your lies
Those lies have worked for you
But sorry isn't worth it anymore

When you came through the door
That morning at a quarter till four
I realized my heart just couldn't take it anymore
It's too late to say you're sorry
Because sorry isn't worth it anymore

It has been almost a year now
Since you pushed me out of the door
My heart still cries for you
And I love you even more
When you called me today
You asked if you could come home
All I could say is I'm sorry
Sorry isn't worth it anymore

Stuck on You

Here I sit eight months later
All I think of is you
I am still so in love with you
I know, to you I mean nothing

I have a love in my heart that is very true
It will not go away
I do not know what to do
I have truly tried to get over you

Everywhere I go and everything I do
I am always thinking of you
My mind knows it's over
But my heart is still very blue

I do not know what it will take
But I need to get over you
Sometimes I think I'm obsessed
I will go to my grave loving you

Take A Chance

With each beat of my heart and every breath I take
I continually wonder what will be my fate
It seems as though my heart is turning to stone
The coldness chills me as I stand alone

It gets tougher each time I try
Harder and colder each time I cry
I want so much to reach out and hold on to you
Within I find it very hard to do

Yet I know if I continue the way I am
I will remain alone with my pain
It is very hard for me to open my heart
I think of the past pain from the very start

I do not know if I should trust in you
Yet if I don't I am certain
I will always be blue

The Battle

I am here walking through the land of death
With no certainty of any future with each and every breath
I look all around me just to see the eyes of despair
Not knowing if we will live or die but a fate we all must share

We muster our strength as we try to put away our fear
At this point and time, the only thing I asked is for God to stand near
Then my mind will wander every night and day
As I try to figure out what it is I will be able to say

The death, the pain, and the misery never seem to go away
It is not the time to be philosophical but why am I here why must I stay
If I were to see their families what would I ever say?

It is three days now since the battle begun
Bayonets are fixed and we thought we had seen our last sun
We yelled our fiercest battle cry and at the enemy, we began to run
We know this was our last battle and for us the was done

All of a sudden from behind me the helicopters had come
The greatest of all battles had finally been overcome
After it is over I look around at all the dead
Will life give me a greater challenge than this that I will dread?

I wonder to myself, why I am still alive when all my friends are dead
It is a loathsome burden that I must carry in my head
Somehow at this moment, I manage to keep my eyes dry
Will it ever be over for me, or will I forever cry?

The Child

When I was little I never knew
What it was I was supposed to do
I needed your guidance
And your patience too

Please stop hitting me
I will be good for you
I am so confused
I am not sure what to do

I thought what I was doing was something good
But it must not have been because you withheld my food
You yelled and scream and hit me some more
Until my little body writhed on the floor

I wanted you to hold me and say it is alright
Instead, you put me in darkness and filled me with fright
Now I am angry and will cry no more
So you can kick me, hit me, and throw me to the floor
My little heart belongs to you no more

The Circle of Love

I traveled the circle, the circle of love
You were my father and towered above
I loved you with all my heart
You were my hero
As I grew, we grew apart
I did not understand you
I got older and grew to understand you
We became close and got to be friends
A few years later you died
Again I love you and you are my hero

The Dark

Is it wrong or is it right?

Will we ever know what is in the darkness without the light?

When I am in the dark and all alone

Isolation is the only zone

Loneliness comes upon me and it will not part

Sometimes it seems eternal from the very start

Being lonely is not all bad

It helps me remember that it's not all sad

I found at my loneliest times

I am not at peace so nothing rhymes

When the light returns and I can see

I noticed that what I did not like has always been me

The Jungle

As we crept through the jungle in the middle of the night
It was darker than dark and fear lingered in the air
I can only imagine on both sides there was a great deal of fright
Life is full of surprises and usually, there is nothing fair

It is funny the thoughts that I had when I was there
Then came the day that I knew I had found my mark
I thought it would feel great because it is why I was there
But I soon realized it will forever keep me in the dark

There are some things that can never be erased from my mind
It does not matter what I do or the justification I use
These ghosts are mine to carry forever throughout time
Now what matters is how I deal with it and the path I choose

Sometimes it still feels as though it were just yesterday
Because the images are still vivid and clear
With the help of my brothers, I have found my way
So now I know forgiveness is mine to have and to share

The Kid

There were no hugs and kisses when I was a kid
My father never said I love you, no matter what I did
I craved it and needed it oh so much
I wantonly craved the feel of his touch

I live my life just to hear a little praise
Mostly looking for someone that would take me to raise
I wanted to hear him call me his son
No matter what I did it was never done

Why can't you see what it is I need?
Keep your money and give me your lead
Spend some time with me and show your love
For I have made you my Hero and placed you above

The most important part of my life
Was taken away and I left in strife
I wanted just once for you to say you were proud
At your funeral, I heard it from your co-worker in the crowd

The Love of a Woman

The love of a woman that is very true
Will lift my soul and keep me from being blue
My nights would seem short and my days fulfilled
All this from the love that is deep and true

When our hearts beat together
No one can set us apart
For love is truly a beautiful work of art
I will love you now and forever until death do us part

The joy our togetherness surely will bring
Will be ours to share forever more
The wondrous feelings shall we sing
The greatest of worth will be our offspring

My heart will fill with sadness no more
For you are the one that I truly adore
From this day forward our love shall be
Written in stone and carved on every tree

The world will know what you mean to me
Our children will grow old and they will see
What true love is through you and me

The Richest Man

How do I measure the wealth in my life?
Is it the new car or having the best wife?
Is it the biggest house and being alone?
Or having great kids and a beautiful home
Can I have millions and really be sad
Can I have nothing and really be glad
How will I measure my success?
It will be by having loved ones that I can caress
If I die and I am alone
Will I be the richest?
Or will you be
With your beautiful home

The Sleeping Giant

You caught America unaware
You thought we were sleeping and would not care
Once again the sleeping giant has been awoke
We will wreak havoc and you may quote
We cherish our freedom and life the most
God help you and to this, we will toast
You have killed our citizens and for this, you will pay
There will be no place for you to hide, or stay
The scales of justice may be blind
However, the eagle's eye is sharp and you he will find
Our people bound together will come to arms
We will rally our battle cry and gather from the farms
Your nightmare has started and of this, you can be sure
No one slaughters our masses, without us finding a cure

The Soldier of War

We are the soldiers of many wars

We all come and stay no matter the length of the tour

We have fought and died in many places

The only things different are the histories, backgrounds, and faces

Our country calls our weary souls

So we pack up and away we go

We dig and live in little holes

Our weapons are loaded and sometimes they glow

The food we eat is not the best

It seems most days we must lay a friend to rest

Most will get mail, some get none at all

But yet we are proud to answer the call

Once again we fight for freedom, to be free evermore

It seems like a vicious cycle of battle and wars

We think the end is somewhere in sight

But history proves it is just another fight

The Special One

May we forever build the special bonds
That ties us together to fight life's storms
May we grow to have that special love
That only comes from God above
With this, I give my love to you
Hold me tight and always be true

Thoughts of You

I am consumed with thoughts of you
It makes the day seem shorter too
When I am sad I think of you
It is as though the sky turns the richest blue

My friends all ask what makes me smile
I say to them I have gone home for a while
The desert heat does not seem so bad
As I remember you and the kiss we had

I am sorry I left but I had to go
All I have now is the memory to show
If I were not so afraid to tell you how I feel
From my mouth, my love would reel

My time here will soon be done
I will then be there at your door
I hope that when I look into your eyes
I will see love and so much more

Time for Me

Time for me shall stand no more
For I have been shown the ultimate door
Love for me shall never be
Why has it taken so long for me to see?
I have this need deep in my heart
Although you say it is not healthy for me it will not part
I'm sorry for the pain and hurt you feel
The hurt and pain for me is real
It is not new to me
It has been my life's companion for all to see

Treasures of the Soul

God has given us some wonderful gifts
Which some will never know
The greatest gift we have received
Is the ability to save our soul

The next of the most wonderful gifts
Is the ability to love and give
For when one gives a heart
It allows another to live

When will we see the signs?
The joy that has been given to us
To choose the path we will take
And the ability to do so without a lot of fuss

For when we give of ourselves
We will surely know
The wonderful feeling in our heart
And how much we are able to grow

God has given us this world
And then His Only Son
It is up to us
To show what can be done

True Strength

True strength is that which comes from within
It cannot be seen or touched
If I look within myself, it is not for me to see
Those around me will see it before I ever do

The outside shell may look so weak
But what is inside may surprise even you
My spiritual strength is my standing Oak
My God is the one that shall carry me

The test of strength is given every day
The biggest Oak looks so strong and tall
Yet the wind can make it topple
And the ground is where it will go

Even I am amazed when faced with diversity
Wonders can be done with conviction and spirituality
With my God, the roots run deep
Forever keeping me tall and straight

Understand

If I could kiss your lips
If I could hold your hand
If I could squeeze you tight
Then you would understand

If you could look into my eyes
If you could feel my heart beat
If you could touch the sweat in my palms
Then you would understand

My love is unconditional
My trust I give to you
My heart is yours to hold
I hope you understand

Time is just a moment
When love is in the plan
My love is yours to have
I hope you understand

Walk with Me

The Lord has asked me to walk with Him
I will be given the knowledge and nourishment
The ability to cope with all adversity
The only requirement is for me to believe

I will know love
Hate will be driven from me
I will see all the beauty
In the mountains and the seas

Life I will come to embrace
As it embraces me
This will all be mine
To last an eternity

To my neighbors, I will be different
As for me, they will also be
That I give my love and truly believe
Is the only thing that is asked of me

Wandering

I wandered aimlessly for many years
My head was full of fog
The fog would not clear

I never knew if what I saw was right
Or was it all a dream
In the middle of the night

My mind was always having a fight
My eyes are heavy, my mind is weary
I tried to sleep but there was too much fright

I would find myself in a light so bright
My body shaking, sweat pouring down
All this in the middle of the night

I find mostly my eyes are full of tears
The ghosts are so real to me, the war is over
It has been eight long years

God, please give some peace
My body is worn and my mind is fried
Let me sleep and my eyes be dry

What Does It Mean

You said you loved me
You said you cared
When I really needed you
You were not there

I needed you to understand
To always be there
To help me through my hard times
Instead, you left me in despair

You turned your back
You said I was the one that did not care
I cried and begged
Hoping you would be there

You walked away
Left me standing here
Now I close my eyes each night
I hope that when I open them
That you will be standing there

Why can't I see?
That your love is not real
Why does my heart stop me
From seeing what is real

What I See

She looks as delicate as the petal of a rose
With all the feminine beauty and charm in the right pose
The glint in her eyes and her coy smile will whisk you away
Be very careful because forever, she will not stay

You give your all because in love you are blind
You hope for her heart and to dwell in her mind
But once again it is proven out with time
She is just another woman that will never be mine

As I struggle to cope with my feeling of loss
She simply moves on to give another man a toss
Whatever happened to the value of family and love
There seems to be no commitment except with the Dove

What is Love

The word love is used so frequently
That it is easy to forget what it actually means
Love is something we do instead of something we feel
Such as having attitudes, patience, actions, and understanding
When we really love we are motivated to act a certain way
Such as making sacrifices for each other
Willing to pitch in and take some of the load
When one is having a poor day
We should have the right to expect that from each other
Once cannot walk the road alone
To have true love we need to have the right attitude
So we take the right actions
If it is all there we will have the right feelings

What The World Can Be

We are the ones that cause the world's destruction
We are the carriers of the world's disease
What will it take for us to learn?
When will we open our eyes and finally see?
We are the ones that cause death and destruction
And continue to destroy the family

Martin had a dream, and then he was destroyed
You can stop the man but the dream lives on
The dream was peace, for all concerned
But after all these years, we still have not learned
We can blame each other, but we all have our own

If we want the world to be different
Then we must be
As long as we continue to stand alone
The world will never be one home

Our hate runs deep and wide
It seems we cannot just reach out
To touch the other side
Maybe it is because we think with our heads
And are unwilling to swallow a little pride

It is so much easier to blame them

Then to open our hearts and really give it a try

My only wish is for the world to see

What a truly wonderful place this could really be

What You Mean to Me

You bring forth a side of me
That I have never displayed for all to see
When I look into your eyes
It is as though they mirror me

There is pain and hurt that I can see
It seems to cause a lot of misery
I can say I'm sorry, that I feel for you
But only you can make your path true

I hope you do not crucify me for all Mans sins
Instead, see me for the loving person I am
Crack your shell and let a little of me in
Then you will know who I am

My eyes are also full of hurt and pain
I will trust you are not the same
My heart will be open for you to share
So come on in and take the dare

What's Missing

Sometimes I feel like the world is passing me by
I wonder why I just sit here and cry
Is pain part of everyday life?
Is there no love just merely sacrifice?
Is the wall I've built so strong and bold?
That it seems like everything outside is so cold
I am all alone on this dreary night
And I know I am not thinking right
I do not know what is real
I only know what I feel

When Death Comes

When death is near and the time is here
The level of understanding becomes very clear
All the things thought to be so important
Are realized to be trivial and not so very dear

The thoughts of all the time wasted
Why did it take death for the truth to be seen?
Thank God for the goodness and a wonderful family
The legacy that is left is in the ones living after me

The curse was all the money and materialistic things
Why did it take death for this to be seen?
The wish that there had been more patience and understanding
That there were more hugs, kisses, and time loving

Thank you, Lord, for the time that is left
Time to share the wisdom before the final test
Hope for the loved ones to open their minds and see
The truly important moments in life are the ones
That come from the heart

Within Me

If you see within my heart
Then you would know from the very start
I have the warmth and love I need
To satisfy you if you are not full of greed
The tenderness that I can show
Will make you smile and your heart will glow
With these words, I hope you see
It is okay to place your trust in me
For I would hold your heart ever so gently
If you could see within my heart
This you would know with certainty

You I see

The largest dam could not hold back my love for you
When you are at my side I feel consumed
With warm and tender thoughts of loving you

I wish I could verbalize the way I feel
There is no measure of time or distance
That could change the feelings I have for you

When I look into your eyes
I am captured for an eternity
A ship floating endlessly on the sea

I hope it is important for you to hear
How much I love you
Throughout the year

My only hope is that you will see
How strong my love forever will be

Your Memory

Every nerve in my body yearned for your touch
You were the one I loved so much
I felt so special when you were near
I had hoped it to last for more than a year
God came along and said it was time
I did not want to believe it, because you were mine

I cuddled with you every night
Trying hard to subdue all the fright
The doctor said you had five years to live
Yet somehow you knew that the time was near
I think I was the one that had the most fear

You smiled and said it would be all right
As I held you tight and cried each night
My heart ached as I held you tight
Knowing that this could be our last night

The hardest thing I have ever done
Was watching you die, as my life went on
Now I am writing this for you
I hope you knew that my love was true

Yours is a memory I shall not forget
The love we had I shall never regret
I only hope when my time comes
That I can be half as brave as you

Your Touch

Your warm smile radiates like the summer sun
Your skin is soft like billowing clouds
The warmth of your breath beckons me
As a flickering fire on a cold winters night
My heart beats wildly when you are near
My love for shall never die
For you are as beautiful as a bright blue sky

www.ingramcontent.com/pod-product-compliance
Lightning Source LLC
Chambersburg PA
CBHW020323130626
46549CB00003B/981